Instructional Guides for Literature

FAHRENHEIT 451

A guide for the novel by Ray Bradbury
Great Works Author: Shelly Buchanan

SHELL EDUCATION

Image Credits

Indigo Fish and Mikhail Bakunovic—Shutterstock (cover)

Standards

© 2007 Teachers of English to Speakers of Other Languages, Inc. (TESOL)
© 2007 Board of Regents of the University of Wisconsin System. World-Class Instructional Design and Assessment (WIDA)
© Copyright 2010 National Governors Association Center for Best Practices and Council of Chief State School Officers.
All rights reserved

Shell Education

5301 Oceanus Drive
Huntington Beach, CA 92649-1030
http://www.shelleducation.com

ISBN 978-1-4258-8992-0

© 2014 Shell Educational Publishing, Inc.

Table of Contents

How to Use This Literature Guide 4

   Theme Thoughts 4

   Vocabulary 5

   Analyzing the Literature 6

   Reader Response 6

   Close Reading the Literature 6

   Making Connections 7

   Creating with the Story Elements 7

   Culminating Activity 8

   Comprehension Assessment 8

   Response to Literature 8

Correlation to the Standards 8

   Purpose and Intent of Standards 8

   How to Find Standards Correlations 8

   Standards Correlation Chart 9

   TESOL and WIDA Standards 10

About the Author—Ray Bradbury 11

   Possible Texts for Text Comparisons 11

   Cross-Curricular Connection 11

Book Summary of *Fahrenheit 451* 12

   Breakdown of the Instructional Guide 12

   Possible Texts for Text Sets 12

Teacher Plans and Student Pages 13

   Pre-Reading Theme Thoughts 13

   Section 1: The First Half of Part One 14

   Section 2: The Second Half of Part One 24

   Section 3: Part Two 34

   Section 4: The First Half of Part Three 44

   Section 5: The Second Half of Part Three 54

Post-Reading Activities 64

   Post-Reading Theme Thoughts 64

   Culminating Activity: Utopia vs. Dystopia 65

   Comprehension Assessment 67

   Response to Literature: Alienation 69

Answer Key 71

How to Use This Literature Guide

Today's standards demand rigor and relevance in the reading of complex texts. The units in this series guide teachers in a rich and deep exploration of worthwhile works of literature for classroom study. The most rigorous instruction can also be interesting and engaging!

Many current strategies for effective literacy instruction have been incorporated into these instructional guides for literature. Throughout the units, text-dependent questions are used to determine comprehension of the book as well as student interpretation of the vocabulary words. The books chosen for the series are complex exemplars of carefully crafted works of literature. Close reading is used throughout the units to guide students toward revisiting the text and using textual evidence to respond to prompts orally and in writing. Students must analyze the story elements in multiple assignments for each section of the book. All of these strategies work together to rigorously guide students through their study of literature.

The next few pages will make clear how to use this guide for a purposeful and meaningful literature study. Each section of this guide is set up in the same way to make it easier for you to implement the instruction in your classroom.

Theme Thoughts

The great works of literature used throughout this series have important themes that have been relevant to people for many years. Many of the themes will be discussed during the various sections of this instructional guide. However, it would also benefit students to have independent time to think about the key themes of the novel.

Before students begin reading, have them complete *Pre-Reading Theme Thoughts* (page 13). This graphic organizer will allow students to think about the themes outside the context of the story. They'll have the opportunity to evaluate statements based on important themes and defend their opinions. Be sure to have students keep their papers for comparison to the *Post-Reading Theme Thoughts* (page 64). This graphic organizer is similar to the pre-reading activity. However, this time, students will be answering the questions from the point of view of one of the characters of the novel. They have to think about how the character would feel about each statement and defend their thoughts. To conclude the activity, have students compare what they thought about the themes before they read the novel to what the characters discovered during the story.

How to Use This Literature Guide (cont.)

Vocabulary

Each teacher overview page has definitions and sentences about how key vocabulary words are used in the section. These words should be introduced and discussed with students. There are two student vocabulary activity pages in each section. On the first page, students are asked to define the ten words chosen by the author of this unit. On the second page in most sections, each student will select at least eight words that he or she finds interesting or difficult. For each section, choose one of these pages for your students to complete. With either assignment, you may want to have students get into pairs to discuss the meanings of the words. Allow students to use reference guides to define the words. Monitor students to make sure the definitions they have found are accurate and relate to how the words are used in the text.

On some of the vocabulary student pages, students are asked to answer text-related questions about the vocabulary words. The following question stems will help you create your own vocabulary questions if you'd like to extend the discussion.

- How does this word describe _____'s character?
- In what ways does this word relate to the problem in this story?
- How does this word help you understand the setting?
- In what ways is this word related to the story's solution?
- Describe how this word supports the novel's theme of . . . .
- What visual images does this word bring to your mind?
- For what reasons might the author have chosen to use this particular word?

At times, more work with the words will help students understand their meanings. The following quick vocabulary activities are a good way to further study the words.

- Have students practice their vocabulary and writing skills by creating sentences and/or paragraphs in which multiple vocabulary words are used correctly and with evidence of understanding.
- Students can play vocabulary concentration. Students make a set of cards with the words and a separate set of cards with the definitions. Then, students lay the cards out on the table and play concentration. The goal of the game is to match vocabulary words with their definitions.
- Students can create word journal entries about the words. Students choose words they think are important and then describe why they think each word is important within the novel.

How to Use This Literature Guide (cont.)

Analyzing the Literature

After students have read each section, hold small-group or whole-class discussions. Questions are written at two levels of complexity to allow you to decide which questions best meet the needs of your students. The Level 1 questions are typically less abstract than the Level 2 questions. Level 1 is indicated by a square, while Level 2 is indicated by a triangle. These questions focus on the various story elements, such as character, setting, and plot. Student pages are provided if you want to assign these questions for individual student work before your group discussion. Be sure to add further questions as your students discuss what they've read. For each question, a few key points are provided for your reference as you discuss the novel with students.

Reader Response

In today's classrooms, there are often great readers who are below average writers. So much time and energy is spent in classrooms getting students to read on grade level, that little time is left to focus on writing skills. To help teachers include more writing in their daily literacy instruction, each section of this guide has a literature-based reader response prompt. Each of the three genres of writing is used in the reader responses within this guide: narrative, informative/explanatory, and argument. Students have a choice between two prompts for each reader response. One response requires students to make connections between the reading and their own lives. The other prompt requires students to determine text-to-text connections or connections within the text.

Close Reading the Literature

Within each section, students are asked to closely reread a short section of text. Since some versions of the novels have different page numbers, the selections are described by chapter and location, along with quotations to guide the readers. After each close reading, there are text-dependent questions to be answered by students.

Encourage students to read each question one at a time and then go back to the text and discover the answer. Work with students to ensure that they use the text to determine their answers rather than making unsupported inferences. Once students have answered the questions, discuss what they discovered. Suggested answers are provided in the answer key.

How to Use This Literature Guide (cont.)

Close Reading the Literature (cont.)

The generic, open-ended stems below can be used to write your own text-dependent questions if you would like to give students more practice.

- Give evidence from the text to support . . . .
- Justify your thinking using text evidence about . . . .
- Find evidence to support your conclusions about . . . .
- What text evidence helps the reader understand . . . ?
- Use the book to tell why _____ happens.
- Based on events in the story, ...
- Use text evidence to describe why . . . .

Making Connections

The activities in this section help students make cross-curricular connections to writing, mathematics, science, social studies, or the fine arts. Each of these types of activities requires higher-order thinking skills from students.

Creating with the Story Elements

It is important to spend time discussing the common story elements in literature. Understanding the characters, setting, and plot can increase students' comprehension and appreciation of the story. If teachers discuss these elements daily, students will more likely internalize the concepts and look for the elements in their independent reading. Another important reason for focusing on the story elements is that students will be better writers if they think about how the stories they read are constructed.

Students are given three options for working with the story elements. They are asked to create something related to the characters, setting, or plot of the novel. Students are given a choice on this activity so that they can decide to complete the activity that most appeals to them. Different multiple intelligences are used so that the activities are diverse and interesting to all students.

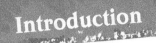

How to Use This Literature Guide (cont.)

Culminating Activity

This open-ended, cross-curricular activity requires higher-order thinking and allows for a creative product. Students will enjoy getting the chance to share what they have discovered through reading the novel. Be sure to allow them enough time to complete the activity at school or home.

Comprehension Assessment

The questions in this section are modeled after current standardized tests to help students analyze what they've read and prepare for tests they may see in their classrooms. The questions are dependent on the text and require critical-thinking skills to answer.

Response to Literature

The final post-reading activity is an essay based on the text that also requires further research by students. This is a great way to extend this book into other curricular areas. A suggested rubric is provided for teacher reference.

Correlation to the Standards

Shell Education is committed to producing educational materials that are research and standards based. As part of this effort, we have correlated all of our products to the academic standards of all 50 states, the District of Columbia, the Department of Defense Dependents Schools, and all Canadian provinces.

Purpose and Intent of Standards

Standards are designed to focus instruction and guide adoption of curricula. Standards are statements that describe the criteria necessary for students to meet specific academic goals. They define the knowledge, skills, and content students should acquire at each level. Standards are also used to develop standardized tests to evaluate students' academic progress. Teachers are required to demonstrate how their lessons meet standards. Standards are used in the development of all of our products, so educators can be assured they meet high academic standards.

How to Find Standards Correlations

To print a customized correlation report of this product for your state, visit our website at http://www.shelleducation.com and follow the online directions. If you require assistance in printing correlation reports, please contact our Customer Service Department at 1-877-777-3450.

Correlation to the Standards (cont.)

Standards Correlation Chart

The lessons in this guide were written to support the Common Core College and Career Readiness Anchor Standards. This chart indicates which sections of this guide address the anchor standards.

Common Core College and Career Readiness Anchor Standard	Section
CCSS.ELA-Literacy.CCRA.R.1—Read closely to determine what the text says explicitly and to make logical inferences from it; cite specific textual evidence when writing or speaking to support conclusions drawn from the text.	Analyzing the Literature Sections 1–5; Close Reading the Literature Sections 1–5; Making Connections Section 4; Creating with the Story Elements Sections 1–5; Culminating Activity; Post-Reading Response to Literature
CCSS.ELA-Literacy.CCRA.R.2—Determine central ideas or themes of a text and analyze their development; summarize the key supporting details and ideas.	Analyzing the Literature Sections 1–5; Making Connections Sections 1–5; Creating with the Story Elements Section 1; Culminating Activity; Post-Reading Response to Literature
CCSS.ELA-Literacy.CCRA.R.3—Analyze how and why individuals, events, or ideas develop and interact over the course of a text.	Analyzing the Literature Sections 1–5; Close Reading the Literature Sections 1–5; Creating with the Story Elements Sections 2, 4; Post-Reading Response to Literature
CCSS.ELA-Literacy.CCRA.R.4—Interpret words and phrases as they are used in a text, including determining technical, connotative, and figurative meanings, and analyze how specific word choices shape meaning or tone.	Vocabulary Sections 1–5
CCSS.ELA-Literacy.CCRA.R.10—Read and comprehend complex literary and informational texts independently and proficiently.	Entire Unit
CCSS.ELA-Literacy.CCRA.W.1—Write arguments to support claims in an analysis of substantive topics or texts using valid reasoning and relevant and sufficient evidence.	Making Connections Sections 3, 5; Creating with the Story Elements Section 5; Reader Response Sections 1, 3, 5
CCSS.ELA-Literacy.CCRA.W.2—Write informative/explanatory texts to examine and convey complex ideas and information clearly and accurately through the effective selection, organization, and analysis of content.	Reader Response Sections 1–4; Making Connections Sections 1–2; Post-Reading Response to Literature; Post-Reading Theme Thoughts
CCSS.ELA-Literacy.CCRA.W.3—Write narratives to develop real or imagined experiences or events using effective technique, well-chosen details and well-structured event sequences.	Creating with the Story Elements Sections 3–5; Reader Response Sections 2, 4–5
CCSS.ELA-Literacy.CCRA.W.4—Produce clear and coherent writing in which the development, organization, and style are appropriate to task, purpose, and audience.	Reader Response Sections 1–5; Making Connections Sections 1, 5; Post-Reading Response to Literature

Correlation to the Standards (cont.)

Standards Correlation Chart (cont.)

Common Core College and Career Readiness Anchor Standard	Section
CCSS.ELA-Literacy.CCRA.W.9—Draw evidence from literary or informational texts to support analysis, reflection, and research.	Making Connections Sections 1–2, 5; Culminating Activity; Post-Reading Response to Literature
CCSS.ELA-Literacy.CCRA.L.1—Demonstrate command of the conventions of standard English grammar and usage when writing or speaking.	Reader Response Sections 1–5; Close Reading the Literature Sections 1–5; Making Connections Sections 1–3, 5; Post-Reading Response to Literature
CCSS.ELA-Literacy.CCRA.L.4—Determine or clarify the meaning of unknown and multiple-meaning words and phrases by using context clues, analyzing meaningful word parts, and consulting general and specialized reference materials, as appropriate.	Vocabulary Sections 1–5
CCSS.ELA-Literacy.CCRA.L.6—Acquire and use accurately a range of general academic and domain-specific words and phrases sufficient for reading, writing, speaking, and listening at the college and career readiness level; demonstrate independence in gathering vocabulary knowledge when encountering an unknown term important to comprehension or expression.	Vocabulary Sections 1–5

TESOL and WIDA Standards

The lessons in this book promote English language development for English language learners. The following TESOL and WIDA English Language Development Standards are addressed through the activities in this book:

- **Standard 1:** English language learners communicate for social and instructional purposes within the school setting.

- **Standard 2:** English language learners communicate information, ideas and concepts necessary for academic success in the content area of language arts.

About the Author—Ray Bradbury

Ray Bradbury credits the traveling circus magician, Mr. Electrico, whom he met at the age of eleven as his first and most memorable inspiration for becoming a writer. After spending an afternoon with the showman discussing magic and philosophies big and small, Bradbury returned home and started writing almost immediately. Bradbury did not stop writing until he died at the age of 92 in 2012. In fact, he claimed that he wrote every single day of his life after meeting the mesmerizing Mr. Electrico.

Bradbury moved around quite a bit with his family as he grew up. He graduated from high school in Los Angeles in 1938. As a student, Bradbury dedicated himself to drama and writing poetry. He planned to become a professional actor. Though he never went to college, Bradbury states that he graduated from the local library at the age of 28, where he spent years educating himself and writing.

Publishing his first short story in a fan magazine called *Imagination!* in 1938, Bradbury enjoyed a 70-year writing career. In 1950, he published a collection of short stories, *The Martian Chronicles*, to wide acclaim and established himself as a science-fiction writer. Soon thereafter, Bradbury started writing for television shows, including *Alfred Hitchcock Presents* and *The Twilight Zone*. Later, he even had his own series called *The Ray Bradbury Theatre*.

In 1950, while living with his family in Venice, California, Bradbury began writing what would become *Fahrenheit 451*. He drafted this novel on pay-by-the-hour typewriters in the basement of the library at the University of California at Los Angeles. The first draft of the novel was complete in nine days and published in *Galaxy Science Fiction* magazine as a short story called "The Fireman." It was published as a full novel in 1953 and became Bradbury's most popular and widely read work. He later produced a stage version of *Fahrenheit 451*. A famous French director created a film adaptation of the novel in 1966.

Bradbury enjoyed a stellar writing career over the course of his lifetime, producing more than 500 publications. He won many awards and honors for his work. In 1980, Bradbury won the Gandalf Award for Lifetime Contribution to Fantasy, and in 2000 he was awarded the Medal for Distinguished Contribution to American Letters by the National Book Foundation.

Possible Texts for Text Comparisons

The Martian Chronicles, *The Illustrated Man*, and *The Stories of Ray Bradbury* are all written by Ray Bradbury and would make good texts for comparison.

Cross-Curricular Connection

This novel is a strong addition to a unit about censorship and government control, which are still relevant topics current today in the United States and around the world.

Book Summary of *Fahrenheit 451*

Fahrenheit 451 is the story of Guy Montag, who is a fireman who doesn't put out fires but starts them. He lives in a futuristic society where he and his fellow firemen make emergency runs when books, now illegal, are discovered.

In "The Hearth and the Salamander," Montag meets his neighbor Clarisse, a teenager who loves to think about ideas and things. Clarisse intrigues Montag, and he begins to think about things in a new way and ask basic questions about how people live. At home, Montag talks with his wife, Mildred, who is confused by Montag's musings. She spends most days watching television on wall-sized screens. Montag grows increasingly uneasy. He even steals books from the scenes of emergencies to try to figure out what it is that is considered dangerous. Montag's boss, Beatty, senses trouble.

In "The Sieve and the Sand," Montag recalls an engaging conversation he once had in a park with a man named Faber. Montag decides he must find Faber again. Faber shares with Montag the power of books to feed and elevate the human spirit, and they decide to work together. An alarm sounds and the firemen race to find the home they will burn. It turns out to be Montag's own home!

In "Burning Bright," Montag turns on Beatty, incinerating him, as well as the Mechanical Hound, a robot programmed to destroy Montag. With Faber's help, Montag escapes from the city with another, more powerful Mechanical Hound on his trail. It's not long before Montag meets a group of intellectuals hiding in the woods led by a man named Granger. Montag learns these men joined together to save knowledge by preserving the books they love; each has memorized a particular beloved book. The novel ends as Montag, invited into the group, watches the city leveled by aerial bombing, while reciting the *Book of Ecclesiastes* from the *Bible*. The men vow to return to the city to rebuild civilization with all the words and ideas they have archived in their hearts and minds.

Breakdown of the Instructional Guide

This novel has three long parts. To study the novel, this guide has the following sections:

- Section 1 is the First Half of Part One, "The Hearth and the Salamander," ending with Montag's last conversation with Clarisse.
- Section 2 is the Second Half of Part One, "The Hearth and the Salamander."
- Section 3 is Part Two, "The Sieve and the Sand."
- Section 4 is the First Half of Part Three, "Burning Bright," ending when Faber and Montag say good-bye to one another.
- Section 5 is the Second Half of Part Three, "Burning Bright."

Possible Texts for Text Sets

- Card, Orson Scott. *Ender's Game*. Tor Science Fiction, 1994.
- Huxley, Aldous. *Brave New World*. Harper Perennial Modern Classic, 2006.
- Orwell, George. *1984*. Signet Classics, 1950.
- Vonnegut, Kurt. *Cat's Cradle*. Dell Publishing, 1998.

Name _____

Date _____

Pre-Reading Theme Thoughts

Directions: Read each of the statements in the first column. Decide if you agree or disagree with the statements. Record your opinion by marking an **X** in the Agree or Disagree box for each statement. Explain your choices in the fourth column. There are no right or wrong answers.

Statement	Agree	Disagree	Explain Your Answer
Watching the news is a good source of information on the key issues of the day.			
Government control of its citizens is important to reduce conflict and violence.			
Knowing how to think about something is more important than knowing how to do something.			
Reading great books is important for a person's general understanding and happiness.			

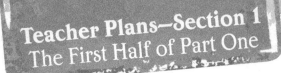
Vocabulary Overview

Ten key words from this section are provided below with definitions and sentences about how the words are used in the book. Choose one of the vocabulary activity sheets (pages 15 or 16) for students to complete as they read this section. Monitor students as they work to ensure the definitions they have found are accurate and relate to the text. Finally, discuss these important vocabulary words with students. If you think these words or other words in the section warrant more time devoted to them, there are suggestions in the introduction for other vocabulary activities (page 5).

Word or Phrase	Definition	Sentence about Text
stolid (part 1)	having or expressing little or no sensibility; unemotional	His **stolid** head held high, Montag flicks the igniter.
suspended (part 1)	supported or kept from sinking or falling by buoyancy or without apparent attachment	Montag sees himself **suspended** in Clarisse's eyes.
accusing (part 1)	blaming for something wrong or illegal	Montag shoots Clarisse **accusing** glances as they walk.
fringe (part 1)	the outside boundary or surface of something	Mildred's breathing stirs only the **fringes** of life.
impersonal (part 1)	having or showing no interest in individual people or their feelings	The **impersonal** operator pumps Mildred's stomach to save her life.
melancholy (part 1)	mournful; depressed	The operators carry their cases of liquid **melancholy** and exit Montag's house.
earnestly (part 1)	serious in intention, purpose, or effort	Clarisse's uncle smiles quietly and **earnestly**.
illuminate (part 1)	brighten with light; light up	The Mechanical Hound sleeps in a dimly **illuminated** kennel.
proboscis (part 1)	the long, thin snout of some animals; any long flexible snout	The **proboscis** of the Mechanical Hound shoots out like a switchblade.
abstract (part 1)	relating to or involving general ideas or qualities rather than specific people, objects, or actions	The image is **abstract**, with no recognizable structure at all.

Name _____

Date _____

Understanding Vocabulary Words

Directions: The following words appear in this section of the book. Use context clues and reference materials to determine an accurate definition for each word.

Word or Phrase	Definition
stolid (part 1)	
suspended (part 1)	
accusing (part 1)	
fringe (part 1)	
impersonal (part 1)	
melancholy (part 1)	
earnestly (part 1)	
illuminate (part 1)	
proboscis (part 1)	
abstract (part 1)	

Name _____

Date _____

During-Reading Vocabulary Activity

Directions: As you read these chapters, record at least eight important words on the lines below. Try to find interesting, difficult, intriguing, special, or funny words. Your words can be long or short. They can be hard or easy to spell. After each word, use context clues in the text and reference materials to define the word.

- _____

- _____

- _____

- _____

- _____

- _____

- _____

- _____

- _____

- _____

Directions: Respond to these questions about the words in this section.

1. In what ways is Clarisse **earnest** when she talks with Montag?

    _____

    _____

2. For what reasons might the Mechanical Hound growl and flick its **proboscis** toward Montag at the fire station?

    _____

    _____

Analyzing the Literature

Provided below are discussion questions you can use in small groups, with the whole class, or for written assignments. Each question is given at two levels so you can choose the right question for each group of students. Activity sheets with these questions are provided (pages 18–19) if you want students to write their responses. For each question, a few key discussion points are provided for your reference.

Story Element	■ Level 1	▲ Level 2	Key Discussion Points
Character	Describe the relationship between Montag and Clarisse.	What is the connection between Montag and Clarisse? How and why does Clarisse intrigue Montag?	Montag sees and is intrigued by Clarisse's curiosity (she asks lots of questions), aliveness (she likes to walk in the rain and stay up all night), and uniqueness from the other people he knows. Clarisse is interested in knowing if Montag is happy. She is curious about him and enjoys that he is willing to talk with her.
Setting	What details or scenes in the novel show how Bradbury envisioned the future?	How does Bradbury create a futuristic society?	This story was written in the early 1950s and is set in a futuristic society. Note that the firemen go up poles as well as down them. Point to the role of firemen as workers who create fires rather than extinguish them. Reference the Mechanical Hound and the parlor walls.
Plot	What emergency happens to Mildred in the middle of the night?	What is Bradbury showing about Mildred with the emergency in the middle of the night?	Mildred overdoses on pain-relieving pills and the medics show up to pump the pills out of her stomach. Discuss how Mildred has no memory of her medical emergency. She is more interested in her parlor walls and the "friends" there that she interacts with every day. Mildred presents a stark contrast to the very human, intelligent, and inquisitive Clarisse.

Name _____

Date _____

Analyzing the Literature

Directions: Think about the section you just read. Read each question and state your response with textual evidence.

1. Describe the relationship between Montag and Clarisse.

_____

_____

_____

_____

_____

2. What details or scenes in the novel show how Bradbury envisioned the future?

_____

_____

_____

_____

_____

3. What emergency happens to Mildred in the middle of the night?

_____

_____

_____

_____

_____

Name _____

Date _____

▲ Analyzing the Literature

Directions: Think about the section you just read. Read each question and state your response with textual evidence.

1. What is the connection between Montag and Clarisse? How and why does Clarisse intrigue Montag?

_____

_____

_____

_____

_____

2. How does Bradbury create a futuristic society?

_____

_____

_____

_____

3. What is Bradbury showing about Mildred with the emergency in the middle of the night?

_____

_____

_____

_____

_____

Name _____

Date _____

Reader Response

Directions: Choose one of the following prompts about this section to answer. Be sure you include a topic sentence in your response, use textual evidence to support your opinion, and provide a strong conclusion that summarizes your opinion.

Writing Prompts

- **Argument Piece**—Over the decades, many books have been challenged and some have been banned from public school libraries. Imagine you have written a book with explicit language, revolutionary ideas, or other controversial content. Write a letter to the school board explaining why your book should not be pulled from the shelves.

- **Informative/Explanatory Piece**—Compare and contrast Clarisse and Mildred with respect to how they each choose to spend their time and how they relate to Montag.

_____

_____

_____

_____

_____

_____

_____

_____

_____

_____

_____

_____

Name _____

Date _____

Close Reading the Literature

Directions: Closely reread the section in "The Hearth and the Salamander" when Montag and Clarisse talk for the third time. Start with, "'Why is it,' he said, 'one time at the subway entrance . . . .'" Read until they each say good-bye. Read each question and then revisit the text to find evidence that supports your answer.

1. Use text examples to illustrate the growing relationship between Montag and Clarisse.

   _____

   _____

   _____

2. Based on what Clarisse tells Montag in this passage, how do you think the society in this story defines a person who is social?

   _____

   _____

   _____

3. According to Clarisse, she is antisocial. Use the text to explain why she doesn't have any friends her own age.

   _____

   _____

   _____

4. Clarisse refers to her uncle several times. What is it that Clarisse has learned from him? Use the text to support your answer.

   _____

   _____

   _____

Name _____

Date _____

Making Connections—The Power of Government

Directions: The power of the United States government has been a significant concern of many people since the founding of the nation in 1776. It is an ongoing challenge for the government to provide programs and resources for its citizens in 50 states while also protecting individual freedoms and rights. Discuss this idea with your family members, asking them about their experiences of government support and times when they experienced too much government control. Using family stories, news stories, and your own ideas, answer the questions below.

1. What do people living in society need from their government?

   _____

   _____

   _____

2. How can people ensure that the government hears the voices of its people and takes seriously and fairly considers their ideas?

   _____

   _____

   _____

3. What kinds of rights do people have today that the people living in the novel's society do not enjoy?

   _____

   _____

   _____

4. What are some current issues of government control that Bradbury might include if he were writing *Fahrenheit 451* today?

   _____

   _____

Creating with the Story Elements

Directions: Thinking about the story elements of character, setting, and plot in a novel is very important to understanding what is happening and why. Complete **one** of the following activities based on what you've read so far. Be creative and have fun!

Characters

Clarisse talks quite poetically about how she lives in the world and what she pays attention to. Using Clarisse's voice, write a poem of 20 lines or more about her fascination with Guy Montag. If possible, post your poem on a fan fiction social media site.

Setting

Choose a key scene from the novel to illustrate using creative software (e.g., *Photoshop®*, *Microsoft Paint®*), colored pencils, pastels, oil, or acrylic paint. Be sure to show through your illustration the qualities of mood and space Bradbury attempted to convey through his descriptions.

Plot

With a partner or in a small group, brainstorm 5–8 predictions for next developments in the novel. Use a graphic organizer, such as a mind map, to support your freethinking. Some categories might be "Relationship between Mildred and Montag," "Montag's feelings and ideas," or "Clarisse and her family." Create a poster (digital or paper) showing your ideas. Share your poster with the class.

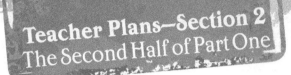
Vocabulary Overview

Ten key words from this section are provided below with definitions and sentences about how the words are used in the book. Choose one of the vocabulary activity sheets (pages 25 or 26) for students to complete as they read this section. Monitor students as they work to ensure the definitions they have found are accurate and relate to the text. Finally, discuss these important vocabulary words with students. If you think these words or other words in the section warrant more time devoted to them, there are suggestions in the introduction for other vocabulary activities (page 5).

Word or Phrase	Definition	Sentence about Text
proclivities (part 1)	natural inclinations or tendencies	Montag wonders if all firemen are hired for their **proclivities**.
odious (part 1)	arousing or deserving hatred; detestable	The firemen run up the sidewalk, suddenly **odious** and fat in their uniforms.
objectivity (part 1)	based on facts rather than feelings or opinions	Beatty slaps the woman's face with amazing **objectivity**.
accusation (part 1)	a charge of wrongdoing	The woman's silence makes the rooms roar with **accusation**.
dignity (part 1)	the quality or state of being worthy, honored, or respected	Captain Beatty keeps his **dignity** by backing through the front door when the woman pulls out a match.
contempt (part 1)	the feeling that someone or something is not worthy of respect or approval	The woman lights the match in **contempt** of all of them.
luminescent (part 1)	the emission of light that does not include processes using heat	To Montag, the idea of the Mechanical Hound is like a faint drift of **luminescent** smoke.
equate (part 1)	to make equal; equalize	Beatty states that the universe cannot be **equated** without making man feel bestial and lonely.
torrent (part 1)	a tumultuous outpouring; rush	Beatty warns Montag not to let the **torrent** of melancholy drown their world.
bewilder (part 1)	to confuse or puzzle completely; perplex	Montag begins to nudge his books, **bewilderedly**, with his hand.

Name _____

Date _____

Understanding Vocabulary Words

Directions: The following words appear in this section of the book. Use context clues and reference materials to determine an accurate definition for each word.

Word or Phrase	Definition
proclivities (part 1)	
odious (part 1)	
objectivity (part 1)	
accusation (part 1)	
dignity (part 1)	
contempt (part 1)	
luminescent (part 1)	
equate (part 1)	
torrent (part 1)	
bewilder (part 1)	

Name _____

Date _____

During-Reading Vocabulary Activity

Directions: As you read these chapters, record at least eight important words on the lines below. Try to find interesting, difficult, intriguing, special, or funny words. Your words can be long or short. They can be hard or easy to spell. After each word, use context clues in the text and reference materials to define the word.

- _____
- _____
- _____
- _____
- _____
- _____
- _____
- _____
- _____
- _____

Directions: Respond to these questions about these words in this section.

1. Beatty talks with the **bewildered** Montag about what happened to Clarisse and her family. What is his explanation?

   _____

   _____

2. According to Clarisse's uncle, the authorities found front porches to be **odious** and directed architects to eliminate them. Why?

   _____

   _____

Analyzing the Literature

Provided below are discussion questions you can use in small groups, with the whole class, or for written assignments. Each question is given at two levels so you can choose the right question for each group of students. Activity sheets with these questions are provided (pages 28–29) if you want students to write their responses. For each question, a few key discussion points are provided for your reference.

Story Element	■ Level 1	▲ Level 2	Key Discussion Points
Character	In the card game at the fire station, Montag asks a number of questions. What kinds of things is Montag trying to learn and understand?	What does Beatty notice about Montag's thinking and ideas during the card game?	Montag is showing concern for a man arrested the week before and registering empathy for those whose houses and books are burned. Montag also references fairy tales and asks about the history of firemen and their role. Beatty's suspicion of Montag is building.
Setting	The firemen are called to incinerate the home and books of an old woman. Describe this woman's home using the text for support.	The home of the old woman is strikingly distinct from the firehouse. Compare the two different settings using examples from the text.	The firehouse is cold and harsh and has the droning "time-voice"; the ticking of the cards; bright, glaring lights; the hum of a radio; and the roaring of jet planes overhead. The woman's home with a lawn and porch shows signs of humanity, including books with words "delicately painted" and heaps of magazines.
Character	Montag and Mildred are growing further apart. Show examples of this using the text.	As Montag grapples with new thoughts and ideas, he becomes increasingly aware of Mildred's emptiness. Using examples from the text, discuss the growing gulf between the married couple.	Students may note Mildred's commitment to her parlor "family" and the seashell she wears in her ear at all times. Mildred cannot remember when and where she and Montag first met. Mildred forgets to mention that Clarisse died. She takes drugs every night and babbles.
Plot	Why does Montag get "sick" and need to take time off work?	What is the significance of Montag's "illness"? How might this shift the plot line?	Montag is made sick by his wife, the burned woman, the loss of Clarisse, the parlor family, violence, and being on the brink of war. His illness will further concern Beatty.

Name _____

Date _____

◼ Analyzing the Literature

Directions: Think about the section you just read. Read each question and state your response with textual evidence.

1. In the card game at the fire station, Montag asks a number of questions. What kinds of things is Montag trying to learn and understand?

_____

_____

_____

_____

2. The firemen are called to incinerate the home and books of an old woman. Describe this woman's home using the text for support.

_____

_____

_____

_____

3. Montag and Mildred are growing further apart. Show examples of this using the text.

_____

_____

_____

_____

4. Why does Montag get "sick" and need to take time off work?

_____

_____

_____

Name _____

Date _____

▲ Analyzing the Literature

Directions: Think about the section you just read. Read each question and state your response with textual evidence.

1. What does Beatty notice about Montag's thinking and ideas during the card game?

   _____

   _____

   _____

   _____

2. The home of the old woman is strikingly distinct from the firehouse. Compare the two different settings using examples from the text.

   _____

   _____

   _____

   _____

3. As Montag grapples with new thoughts and ideas, he becomes increasingly aware of Mildred's emptiness. Using examples from the text, discuss the growing gulf between the married couple.

   _____

   _____

   _____

4. What is the significance of Montag's "illness"? How might this shift the plotline?

   _____

   _____

   _____

Name _____

Date _____

Reader Response

Directions: Choose one of the following prompts about this section to answer. Be sure you include a topic sentence in your response, use textual evidence to support your opinion, and provide a strong conclusion that summarizes your opinion.

Writing Prompts

- **Information/Explanatory Piece**—In the novel, television projected on the parlor walls is a popular pastime offering quick and easy entertainment to most of the city's people. The shows Mildred watches are similar to the reality TV programs so popular today. How close or far are we from enjoying the kinds of "families" Mildred claims to love so much?

- **Narrative Piece**—Imagine if the old woman who burns herself up in her home with her books had a chance to explain herself to Montag. Write a scene in which she shares her story and why books are such a central part of her life.

_____

_____

_____

_____

_____

_____

_____

_____

_____

_____

_____

_____

Close Reading the Literature

Directions: Closely reread the section toward the end of "The Hearth and the Salamander" in which Beatty visits Montag at home in bed. Begin reading with, "When did it all start . . . ." End with, "He turned and went out . . . ." Read each question and then revisit the text to find evidence that supports your answer.

1. According to Beatty, what happened to books and magazines in the 20th century, and why?

   _____

   _____

   _____

2. While Beatty is in the room, Mildred finds the book Montag hid behind his pillow. Use text evidence to describe how she reacts.

   _____

   _____

   _____

3. Beatty says that civilization cannot have minorities upset. Use the text to describe the reasoning behind this idea.

   _____

   _____

   _____

4. What kinds of things does Montag's society provide to keep people happy? Use the text to explain if these things actually do keep people happy.

   _____

   _____

   _____

Name _____

Date _____

Making Connections—Censorship

Directions: Talk with your family and friends about their opinions of censorship and books that have been banned in the past. Learn why certain books have been banned in some places. Take what you learn and apply your thoughts, ideas, and opinions to answer the following questions.

1. Based on the story so far, what do you believe is Bradbury's perspective on censorship?

   _____

   _____

   _____

2. For what reasons do you think that freedom of expression is specifically noted in the First Amendment to the United States Constitution?

   _____

   _____

   _____

3. Are there any ideas from which people need to be protected? Explain using specific examples.

   _____

   _____

   _____

4. Explain how people can benefit from learning about ideas and values very different from their own.

   _____

   _____

   _____

Name _____

Date _____

Creating with the Story Elements

Directions: Thinking about the story elements of character, setting, and plot in a novel is very important to understanding what is happening and why. Complete **one** of the following activities based on what you've read so far. Be creative and have fun!

Characters

Create a comic strip showing Montag and Mildred on a date after first meeting each other. Be sure to stay true to some elements of their character, recognizing their relationship may have been quite different at the start.

Setting

Create an illustration (digital, collage, drawing, or painting) of the interior of the McClellan home when Clarisse and her family lived there.

Plot

Using events, characters, themes, and descriptions of the story so far, create a poster on or a three-dimensional box showing the most intriguing and important developments in the story so far. You might include any notable predictions you have about certain aspects of the story.

Vocabulary Overview

Ten key words from this section are provided below with definitions and sentences about how the words are used in the book. Choose one of the vocabulary activity sheets (pages 35 or 36) for students to complete as they read this section. Monitor students as they work to ensure the definitions they have found are accurate and relate to the text. Finally, discuss these important vocabulary words with students. If you think these words or other words in the section warrant more time devoted to them, there are suggestions in the introduction for other vocabulary activities (page 5).

Word or Phrase	Definition	Sentence about Text
sieve (part 2)	a strainer for separating smaller particles from larger ones	Montag had once tried to fill a **sieve** with sand, but it was impossible.
subside (part 2)	to become less strong or intense	Montag waits for the shock of hearing about Clarisse's death to **subside** before opening another book.
insidious (part 2)	intended to entrap or beguile	Montag and Faber's plan is an **insidious** one, but it would get the job done.
devours (part 2)	eats up greedily or ravenously	Faber describes the plan to burn firemen's houses as, "The salamander **devours** his tail!"
dispersing (part 2)	to drive or send off in various directions; distribute loosely	Mildred **disperses** the dynamite (i.e., books) in her house one by one.
filigree (part 2)	anything delicate or fanciful	The **filigree** quality of Faber's voice sounds good to Montag.
invigorated (part 2)	filled with life or energy; energized	Montag's anger **invigorates** Faber, who is listening on the earpiece.
manifest (part 2)	to make clear or evident; to show plainly	Montag feels guilty that his conscience **manifested** itself and stole books.
rebut (part 2)	to refute by evidence, argument, or proof	Beatty uses books to **rebut** every point Montag is thinking about.
beatific (part 2)	experiencing or bestowing celestial joy	Beatty paints an image of riding on the salamander in **beatific** silence.

Name _____

Date _____

Understanding Vocabulary Words

Directions: The following words appear in this section of the book. Use context clues and reference materials to determine an accurate definition for each word.

Word or Phrase	Definition
sieve (part 2)	
subside (part 2)	
insidious (part 2)	
devours (part 2)	
dispersing (part 2)	
filigree (part 2)	
invigorated (part 2)	
manifest (part 2)	
rebut (part 2)	
beatific (part 2)	

Name _____

Date _____

During-Reading Vocabulary Activity

Directions: As you read these chapters, record at least eight important words on the lines below. Try to find interesting, difficult, intriguing, special, or funny words. Your words can be long or short. They can be hard or easy to spell. After each word, use context clues in the text and reference materials to define the word.

- _____

- _____

- _____

- _____

- _____

- _____

- _____

- _____

- _____

Directions: Now, organize your words. Rewrite each of your words on a sticky note. Work as a group to create a bar graph of your words. You should stack any words that are the same on top of one another. Different words appear in different columns. Finally, discuss with your group why certain words were chosen more often than other words.

Analyzing the Literature

Provided below are discussion questions you can use in small groups, with the whole class, or for written assignments. Each question is given at two levels so you can choose the right question for each group of students. Activity sheets with these questions are provided (pages 38–39) if you want students to write their responses. For each question, a few key discussion points are provided for your reference.

Story Element	■ Level 1	▲ Level 2	Key Discussion Points
Setting	On the subway, what happens when Montag hears the advertisement for Denham's Dentifrice?	What does Bradbury try to show the reader in the subway scene about Montag, his pursuits, and the society in which he lives?	Montag's attempt to read, consider, and memorize a portion of the Bible is interrupted by the blaring advertisement. The culture discourages people from thinking about ideas and their meaning. Montag shows his rage to the other passengers, who then call for the authorities.
Character	What are Faber's beliefs about books and their importance?	What is significant about Faber's comments on the importance of books?	Faber believes that books contain ideas, knowledge, history, and emotion. It is the meaning in books that is important. People need the time to read, think about, and act upon the ideas they discover.
Plot	What happens in the scene where Montag reads *Dover Beach* aloud to Mildred and her friends?	Why does Montag read *Dover Beach* to the three women? How do they respond, and why?	Students may highlight Montag's attempt to startle the women with thoughts of lost faith and the destruction of war and lies. The women become quite upset by the disturbing ideas. They resist thinking about ideas, feelings, and truth.
Character	How does Beatty attempt to dissuade Montag from his fascination with books?	What do we learn about Beatty in his speech about books to Montag?	Beatty attempts to scare Montag, who he sees is wavering and confused, with words and ideas from books to show the many conflicting ideas within books. Beatty wants to show how upsetting books and their ideas can be for people who do not resist them.

Name _____

Date _____

Analyzing the Literature

Directions: Think about the section you just read. Read each question and state your response with textual evidence.

1. On the subway, what happens when Montag hears the advertisement for Denham's Dentifrice?

_____

_____

_____

_____

2. What are Faber's beliefs about books and their importance?

_____

_____

_____

_____

3. What happens in the scene where Montag reads *Dover Beach* aloud to Mildred and her friends?

_____

_____

_____

_____

4. How does Beatty attempt to dissuade Montag from his fascination with books?

_____

_____

_____

Name _____

Date _____

▲ Analyzing the Literature

Directions: Think about the section you just read. Read each question and state your response with textual evidence.

1. What does Bradbury try to show the reader in the subway scene about Montag, his pursuits, and the society in which he lives?

_____

_____

_____

_____

2. What is significant about Faber's comments on the importance of books?

_____

_____

_____

_____

3. Why does Montag read *Dover Beach* to the three women? How do they respond, and why?

_____

_____

_____

_____

4. What do we learn about Beatty in his speech about books to Montag?

_____

_____

_____

_____

Name _____

Date _____

Reader Response

Directions: Choose one of the following prompts about this section to answer. Be sure you include a topic sentence in your response, use textual evidence to support your opinion, and provide a strong conclusion that summarizes your opinion.

Writing Prompts

- **Information/Explanatory Piece**—According to Faber there are three things required for the achievement of happiness—books and reading, leisure to wonder and think, and the ability to act on your thoughts and ideas. In what ways do you agree with Faber? If you don't agree, explain what you believe are the three requirements for happiness.

- **Argument Piece**—Why is reading important? Imagine that our government banned reading entirely. Write an op-ed piece for a newspaper or a blog post in defense of reading. Start by brainstorming a list of the benefits that come from reading.

_____

_____

_____

_____

_____

_____

_____

_____

_____

_____

_____

Close Reading the Literature

Directions: Closely reread the section in which Faber and Montag philosophize about books and society. Start with, "It's been a long time." Read through, ". . . at least die knowing you were headed for shore." Read each question and then revisit the text to find evidence that supports your answer.

1. Use text evidence to describe how Faber describes his failure as a citizen .

   _____

   _____

   _____

2. Explain the three things people need in order to thrive, according to Faber.

   _____

   _____

   _____

3. Based on the novel, why do most people in *Fahrenheit 451* hate and fear books?

   _____

   _____

   _____

4. Explain what Faber means when he says to Montag, "We are living in a time when flowers are trying to live on flowers, instead of growing on good rain and black loam."

   _____

   _____

   _____

   _____

Name _____

Date _____

Making Connections–The Ingredients for a Healthy Society

Directions: Are there basic requirements for a fully functioning and relatively contented community, society, or nation? Research to build background knowledge, answer the questions below, and then compose your own proposal for a successful society.

1. Talk with three people—friends, teachers, or family members—and ask them what they think are the most important components of a healthy society, and why. List them here.

   _____

   _____

   _____

   _____

2. Research to find an ancient civilization or society considered to have been successful. Explain their successes.

   _____

   _____

   _____

3. Explain the strengths and weaknesses of society today.

   _____

   _____

   _____

   _____

4. On another sheet of paper, describe what you believe to be the necessary ingredients for a healthy society.

Name _____

Date _____

Creating with the Story Elements

Directions: Thinking about the story elements of character, setting, and plot in a novel is very important to understanding what is happening and why. Complete **one** of the following activities based on what you've read so far. Be creative and have fun!

Characters

Assume the character of Mildred. Write a blog entry where Mildred reflects upon the scene when Montag turns off the parlor walls and attempts to engage Mildred and her two friends in a conversation about politics, family, and the impending war. Be sure to include the part where Montag reads aloud from *Dover Beach*.

Setting

Reread the subway passage that includes the Denham's Dentifrice loudspeaker advertisement. Create an advertising campaign for another product offered on both the loudspeaker and the walls of the subway. Draft the voice-over monologue for the product as a podcast or in writing. Create a two-dimensional visual using your choice of medium (ink, paint, digital). Be sure this product is appropriate for its Bradbury-created audience.

Plot

Write, perform, and if possible, record a dialogue between two teens on the topic of modern social media. Incorporate the main components Faber claims are necessary for human happiness and satisfaction. Show where social media meets some of these needs and where it falls short.

Vocabulary Overview

Ten key words from this section are provided below with definitions and sentences about how the words are used in the book. Choose one of the vocabulary activity sheets (pages 45 or 46) for students to complete as they read this section. Monitor students as they work to ensure the definitions they have found are accurate and relate to the text. Finally, discuss these important vocabulary words with students. If you think these words or other words in the section warrant more time devoted to them, there are suggestions in the introduction for other vocabulary activities (page 5).

Word or Phrase	Definition	Sentence about Text
rigidity (part 3)	to be stiff and resist bending	Mildred clenches the suitcase handle with great **rigidity** as she runs out the door.
incomprehensible (part 3)	incapable of being explained or understood	Montag watches in an **incomprehensible** stupor as firemen shatter the windows of his home.
rend (part 3)	to tear or be torn violently	It feels good to Montag to **rend** his books with flame.
writhing (part 3)	twisting; contorting; distorting	Beatty **writhes** on the lawn when Montag sets him on fire.
wavering (part 3)	to go back and forth between choices or opinions	The police helicopters flitted about in the air, **wavering** and indecisive.
faltered (part 3)	moved hesitatingly; stopped being strong or successful	Montag **falters** as he is crossing the wide street and hears the speeding beetle.
flailing (part 3)	moving or swinging in a wild or uncontrolled way	Montag's arms and legs are **flailing** about as he scrambles to cross the street.
luminous (part 3)	filled with light; brightly lit	While at Faber's house, Montag's body feels like a **luminous** cloud, ghostlike and breathless.
limn (part 3)	to draw or paint; delineate; describe	**Limned** in life-like proportions, Montag imagines himself on the parlor screens.
douse (part 3)	to throw a liquid on; drench	Montag **douses** a suitcase with whiskey to throw the Mechanical Hound off his scent.

Name _____

Date _____

Understanding Vocabulary Words

Directions: The following words appear in this section of the book. Use context clues and reference materials to determine an accurate definition for each word.

Word or Phrase	Definition
rigidity (part 3)	
incomprehensible (part 3)	
rend (part 3)	
writhing (part 3)	
wavering (part 3)	
faltered (part 3)	
flailing (part 3)	
luminous (part 3)	
limn (part 3)	
douse (part 3)	

Name _____

Date _____

During-Reading Vocabulary Activity

Directions: As you read these chapters, record at least eight important words on the lines below. Try to find interesting, difficult, intriguing, special, or funny words. Your words can be long or short. They can be hard or easy to spell. After each word, use context clues in the text and reference materials to define the word.

- _____
- _____
- _____
- _____
- _____
- _____
- _____
- _____
- _____

Directions: Respond to these questions about the words in this section.

1. **Rending** his relationship with the firefighters Montag hides books in Black's home and sounds the alarm. Why?

   _____

   _____

2. What picture do the authorities hope to **limn** for the public by televising the hunt for Montag?

   _____

   _____

Analyzing the Literature

Provided below are discussion questions you can use in small groups, with the whole class, or for written assignments. Each question is given at two levels so you can choose the right question for each group of students. Activity sheets with these questions are provided (pages 48–49) if you want students to write their responses. For each question, a few key discussion points are provided for your reference.

Story Element	■ Level 1	▲ Level 2	Key Discussion Points
Character	Do you think Beatty wanted to die? Explain your answer using the text.	Bradbury shows the subtleties of character in Montag and Beatty in their final scene together. Why does Montag burn Beatty?	Beatty says that fire "destroys responsibility and commitment" and taunts Montag with lines from Shakespeare and name-calling. Beatty may feel he is in over his head, with no way out of the controlled society he helps manage.
Setting	Why do you think the teenagers try to run Montag down? Use elements from the novel to explain your reasons.	How are the speeding teenagers behaving as typical citizens in this story? Cite the text to support your ideas.	The people in this world look for excitement, without any true commitment to feelings or ideas. The teenagers are looking for a cheap thrill, just as Mildred looked for shallow entertainment from her "family" on the parlor walls.
Theme	If he were caught, what words could Montag cry out in his last moments alive to make an impact and wake up the public?	What do you believe the public needs to realize to spark a revolution against the government?	Montag wishes people to consider the ideas of others, to share ideas and feelings with others, to wonder, to daydream, to philosophize, and to create. Montag wishes people would recognize and enjoy their human qualities, including feelings of pain, pleasure, and connectedness.
Plot	Why must Montag leave town? What does he hope to accomplish?	What do Montag and Faber hope to achieve long term?	Montag is going to follow the railroad tracks out of town and meet up with a group of learned, homeless men. Faber plans to visit his printer friend in St. Louis. They hope for a different future, one with books, ideas, friends, and feelings.

Name _____

Date _____

Analyzing the Literature

Directions: Think about the section you just read. Read each question and state your response with textual evidence.

1. Do you think Beatty wanted to die? Explain your answer using the text.

   _____

   _____

   _____

   _____

2. Why do you think the teenagers try to run Montag down? Use elements from the novel to explain your reasons.

   _____

   _____

   _____

   _____

3. If he were caught, what words could Montag cry out in his last moments alive to make an impact and wake up the public?

   _____

   _____

   _____

   _____

4. Why must Montag leave town? What does he hope to accomplish?

   _____

   _____

   _____

▲ Analyzing the Literature

Directions: Think about the section you just read. Read each question and state your response with textual evidence.

1. Bradbury shows the subtleties of character in Montag and Beatty in their final scene together. Why does Montag burn Beatty?

_____

_____

_____

_____

2. How are the speeding teenagers behaving as typical citizens in this story? Cite the text to support your ideas.

_____

_____

_____

_____

3. What do you believe the public needs to realize to spark a revolution against the government?

_____

_____

_____

_____

4. What do Montag and Faber hope to achieve long term?

_____

_____

_____

Name _____

Date _____

Reader Response

Directions: Choose one of the following prompts about this section to answer. Be sure you include a topic sentence in your response, use textual evidence to support your opinion, and provide a strong conclusion that summarizes your opinion.

Writing Prompts

- **Informative/Explanatory Piece**—We get a brief glimpse of teenagers in this novel with the introduction of Clarisse and later the group of teenagers who try to run down Montag. Compare you and your friends to these characters.
- **Narrative Piece**—Where does Mildred go after calling the authorities on Montag, packing her suitcase, and leaving her home? Write the next scene in Mildred's life. Be sure to stay true to her character and the setting Bradbury has created in the novel.

_____

_____

_____

_____

_____

_____

_____

_____

_____

_____

_____

_____

_____

Close Reading the Literature

Directions: Closely reread the section in part three starting with the opening of the chapter. Read through, "You're under arrest." Read each question and then revisit the text to find evidence that supports your answer.

1. According to the events in the story, why does Mildred leave her house with a suitcase?

   _____

   _____

2. During this scene, how does Beatty describe the power and beauty of fire?

   _____

   _____

3. Identify 2–3 examples of figurative language in this scene. Why does Bradbury use this language? What effects does this have on the reader?

   _____

   _____

   _____

4. Use the text to describe how Montag feels as he burns his home down to the ground.

   _____

   _____

   _____

Name _____

Date _____

Making Connections–Innocent?

Directions: Complete this T-chart to describe what makes Montag guilty of crimes against society and what makes him an innocent victim of his government.

Guilty	Innocent

Name _____

Date _____

Creating with the Story Elements

Directions: Thinking about the story elements of character, setting, and plot in a novel is very important to understanding what is happening and why. Complete **one** of the following activities based on what you've read so far. Be creative and have fun!

Characters

Beatty taunts Montag while Montag holds the fire hose. Does Beatty hope that Montag will burn him? Does Beatty think Montag will not consider flouting his authority? Write an interior monologue for Beatty as he stands there waiting for Montag's response to his admonitions and insults. Stay in character. Show Beatty's innermost thoughts during these moments.

Setting

In this section, a car of teenagers tries to run Montag down for fun. Think of three other scenes that Bradbury could have created to show Montag on the run and also confronting the inhuman behavior typical of the average citizens in the novel. Create storyboards or comic strips to show your ideas.

Plot

The authorities are focused on showing the public how they deal with detractors and lawbreakers. Write 10 tweets issued by the government that show the kinds of things the government wants the public to know about, including Montag's escape and the impending war.

Vocabulary Overview

Ten key words from this section are provided below with definitions and sentences about how the words are used in the book. Choose one of the vocabulary activity sheets (pages 55 or 56) for students to complete as they read this section. Monitor students as they work to ensure the definitions they have found are accurate and relate to the text. Finally, discuss these important vocabulary words with students. If you think these words or other words in the section warrant more time devoted to them, there are suggestions in the introduction for other vocabulary activities (page 5).

Word or Phrase	Definition	Sentence about Text
silhouettes (part 3)	outlines of solid objects	The **silhouettes** of people watching the parlor walls show through the curtained windows as Montag races past.
séance (part 3)	a meeting for communication with spirits	The people watching the hunt for Montag look like they're at **séances**.
juggernaut (part 3)	something that is very powerful and cannot be stopped	While on the river, Montag feels threatened by a great **juggernaut** of stars.
veered (part 3)	changed direction or course	The search for Montag **veers** inland away from Montag.
warily (part 3)	concerned or hesitant; nervous	Montag approaches the fire **warily**.
converging (part 3)	moving or coming together at the same location	The police helicopters **converge** as they continue their fake chase of Montag.
incite (part 3)	to cause to act in an angry, harmful, or violent way	The men on the tracks are not trying to **incite** the public.
pedants (part 3)	people who make a show of their knowledge	The men along the railroad know it is important not to be **pedants** to the rest of society.
resolve (part 3)	to find an answer or solution; to solve	The men walking along the tracks **resolved** to make a difference.
prattled (part 3)	spoke rapidly and continuously	Mildred's "family" **prattles** on to her day after day after day.

Name _____

Date _____

Understanding Vocabulary Words

Directions: The following words appear in this section of the book. Use context clues and reference materials to determine an accurate definition for each word.

Word or Phrase	Definition
silhouettes (part 3)	
séance (part 3)	
juggernaut (part 3)	
veered (part 3)	
warily (part 3)	
converging (part 3)	
incite (part 3)	
pedants (part 3)	
resolve (part 3)	
prattled (part 3)	

Name _____

Date _____

During-Reading Vocabulary Activity

Directions: As you read these chapters, choose five important words from the story. Use these words to complete the word flow chart below. On each arrow, write a word. In each box, explain how the connected pair of words relates to each other. An example for the words *veer* and *converge* has been done for you.

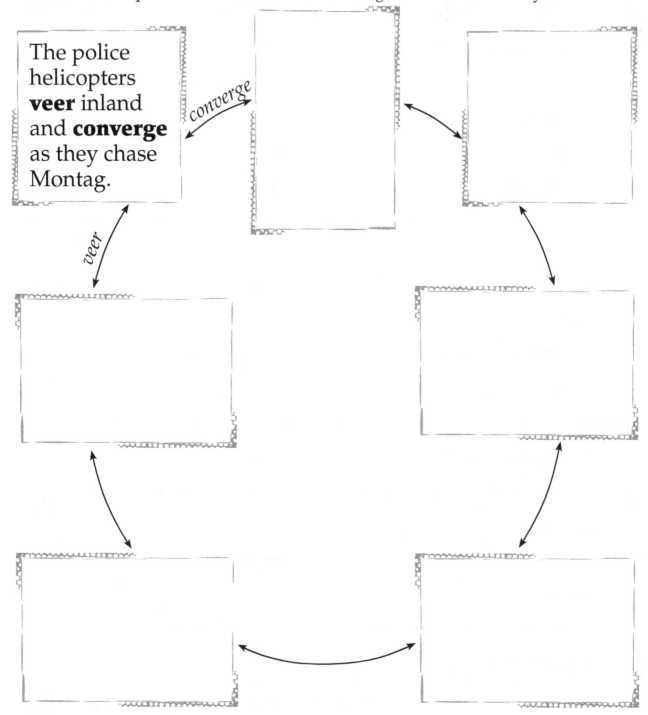

The police helicopters **veer** inland and **converge** as they chase Montag.

converge

veer

Analyzing the Literature

Provided below are discussion questions you can use in small groups, with the whole class, or for written assignments. Each question is given at two levels so you can choose the right question for each group of students. Activity sheets with these questions are provided (pages 58–59) if you want students to write their responses. For each question, a few key discussion points are provided for your reference.

Story Element	■ Level 1	▲ Level 2	Key Discussion Points
Character	Granger introduces each of the homeless men to Montag as titles of books. Why? What impact does this have?	Why have the men memorized books? How do they believe this will be helpful in the future?	The men memorized great works of literature. They believe that a distinguishing feature of humanness is the capacity for ideas, feelings, innovation, and art. They may have a chance to rebuild society.
Theme	Explain why the authorities carry on with the chase even after they know Montag successfully escaped.	Use the text to describe why the authorities stage the "death of Montag" with an innocent man.	The police need to maintain complete authority and control over the people. They must not reveal that Montag has escaped. They sacrifice an innocent man to show that any mutinous behavior will be squelched immediately. In this way, the police are able to keep people, their actions, and their thoughts in check.
Setting	How does the railroad track serve Montag in the closing section of the novel?	Discuss Bradbury's choice of the railroad track as a connection from the story's time to the past. How does the railroad support the story?	Discuss the literal and the metaphorical significances of the railroad. It serves as a real, physical guide to Montag. It also symbolizes the past by taking him to the learned people who hold old ideas. The railroad is both past and future; it brings those together who may challenge the status quo and rebuild a better, brighter future.
Plot	Why are the homeless men gathered together in the forest outside the city?	How does Bradbury suggest optimistic themes by having this group of men banded together?	The men are scholars, professors, and scientists who remember the old days when people shared ideas, grappled with philosophies, and engaged in arts. These men are planning for a new, brighter future. Themes of perseverance, creativity, bravery, and justice may be discussed.

Name _____

Date _____

Analyzing the Literature

Directions: Think about the section you just read. Read each question and state your response with textual evidence.

1. Granger introduces each of the homeless men to Montag as titles of books. Why? What impact does this have?

_____

_____

_____

_____

2. Explain why the authorities carry on with the chase even after they know Montag successfully escaped.

_____

_____

_____

_____

3. How does the railroad track serve Montag in the closing section of the novel?

_____

_____

_____

_____

4. Why are the homeless men gathered together in the forest outside the city?

_____

_____

_____

Name _____

Date _____

▲ Analyzing the Literature

Directions: Think about the section you just read. Read each question and state your response with textual evidence.

1. Why have the men memorized books? How do they believe this will be helpful in the future?

   _____

   _____

   _____

   _____

2. Use the text to describe why the authorities stage the "death of Montag" with an innocent man.

   _____

   _____

   _____

   _____

3. Discuss Bradbury's choice of the railroad track as a connection from the story's time to the past. How does the railroad support the story?

   _____

   _____

   _____

4. How does Bradbury suggest optimistic themes by having this group of men banded together?

   _____

   _____

   _____

Name _____

Date _____

Reader Response

Directions: Choose one of the following prompts about this section to answer. Be sure you include a topic sentence in your response, use textual evidence to support your opinion, and provide a strong conclusion that summarizes your opinion.

Writing Prompts

- **Argument Piece**—If you had to "be" a book like the learned homeless men living in the forest, which book would you choose? Write about a book that has made a difference to you, one you won't ever forget, and one you would defend against censorship were it challenged. What do you love about this book? What impact has it had on you? How might it enlighten others?
- **Narrative Piece**—In the last scene of the novel, Montag leads the group of men toward the city. Write an alternate ending to the story that still seems fitting, or write the opening scene of *Fahrenheit 451, Part II.*

_____

_____

_____

_____

_____

_____

_____

_____

_____

_____

_____

Name _____

Date _____

Close Reading the Literature

Directions: Closely reread the section which begins with, "But he was at the river . . . ." Stop reading with, "He stepped from the river." Read each question and then revisit the text to find evidence that supports your answer.

1. Based on the text, why does Montag get into the river?

   _____

   _____

   _____

2. Describe the kinds of emotions Montag experiences while in the river.

   _____

   _____

   _____

3. For what reasons does Montag decide he must never burn again?

   _____

   _____

   _____

   _____

4. Montag remembers a farm he visited when he was young and fantasizes about staying overnight in a barn. What does he wish to experience by spending time in the countryside, and why?

   _____

   _____

   _____

   _____

Name _____

Date _____

Making Connections—Censoring Books

Directions: Find out about censorship in public high schools. Then, use the Venn diagram to compare and contrast the two sides of the debate. Identify the types of people on each side of the issue, the reasons they state for their positions, any examples they present to fortify their arguments, and counterpoints delivered. After completing the Venn diagram, use another sheet of paper to write about how you personally feel about censoring books in high schools today.

Pro Censorship   Anti Censorship

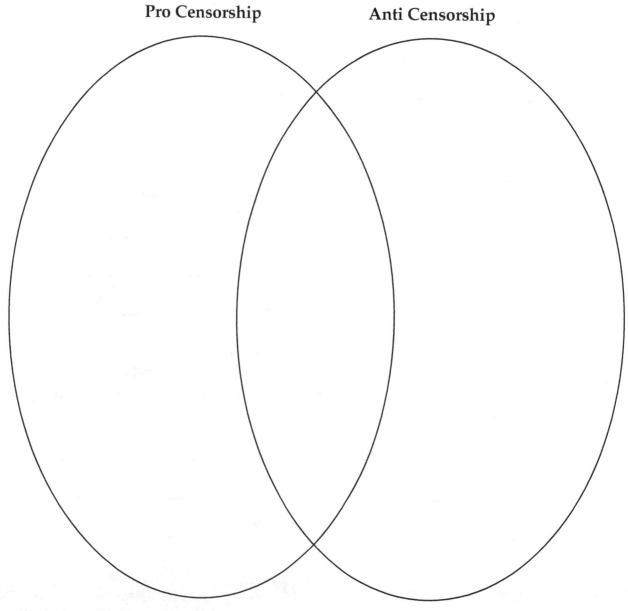

Name _____

Date _____

Creating with the Story Elements

Directions: Thinking about the story elements of character, setting, and plot in a novel is very important to understanding what is happening and why. Complete **one** of the following activities based on what you've read so far. Be creative and have fun!

Characters

As he watches the bombing and flattening of the city, Montag thinks about Mildred, her sad life, and presumed death. Pretend that she survives and that Montag wants to reconnect with her and try their marriage again. Write a letter from Montag to Mildred in which he shows her the possibilities for their future, how they can be in the world together, and what he hopes she would experience and discover in that new life and relationship.

Setting

Montag, Granger, and the other men hope for the rebuilding of the city. Create at least two illustrations (using colored pencils, markers, ink, paint, or digital tools) showing the kind of city you believe these men would hope to see created in place of the one just destroyed. Be sure to include details that reflect the values of this thoughtful, learned group.

Plot

After the bombing of the city, the men head towards the city to support any survivors. Create the front-page of a digital national newspaper about the bombing of the city. Consider including stories about and quotes from other characters, politicians, police, philosophers, artists, etc., about what happened, what led up to the bombing, and any ideas or plans for the near and far future.

Name _____

Date _____

Post-Reading Theme Thoughts

Directions: Read each of the statements in the first column. Choose a main character from *Fahrenheit 451*. Think about that character's point of view. From that character's perspective, decide if the character would agree or disagree with the statements. Record the character's opinion by marking an **X** in the Agree or Disagree box for each statement. Explain your choices in the third column using text evidence.

Character I Chose: _____

Statement	Agree	Disagree	Explain Your Answer
Watching the news is a good source of information on the key issues of the day.			
Government control of its citizens is important to reduce conflict and violence.			
Knowing how to think about something is more important than knowing how to do something.			
Reading great books is important for a person's general understanding and happiness.			

Name _____

Date _____

Culminating Activity: Utopia vs. Dystopia

Directions: With a partner or in a small group, discuss your understandings of utopias and dystopias. Complete this Venn diagram detailing the characteristics of each type of society. Circle or highlight any characteristics found in *Fahrenheit 451*. Compare and discuss your findings with your classmates.

Utopias   **Dystopias**

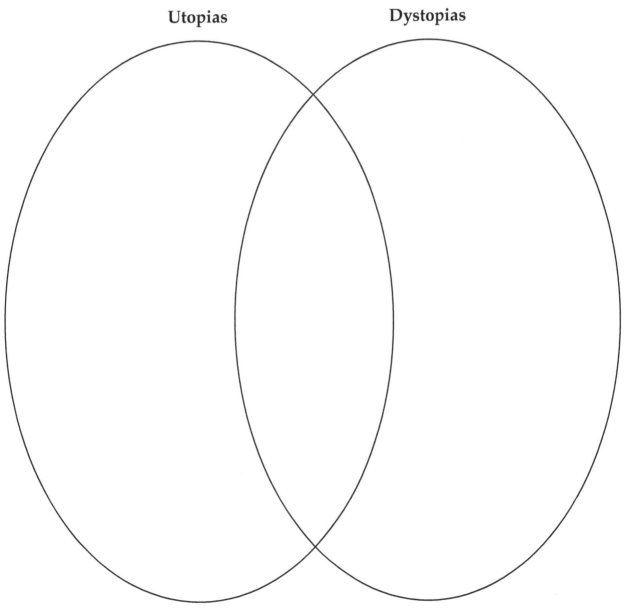

Name _____

Date _____

Culminating Activity:
Utopia vs. Dystopia *(cont.)*

Directions: Using what you've discovered about utopias and dystopias, write an illustrated poem about these created societies. Collect your favorite words and phrases from the novel and your Venn diagram. Assemble the pieces of language artfully to reflect ideas about a particular character, a theme, or a moment in these types of novels.

Name _____

Date _____

Comprehension Assessment

Directions: Circle the letter for the best response to each question.

1. What statement best supports the reason books are illegal in *Fahrenheit 451*?

    A. Reading takes up too much time.

    B. Books offer a range of ideas and perspectives, some conflicting.

    C. Readers need to engage in more challenging material.

    D. Books are too expensive to print.

2. What detail from the book best supports your answer to question 1?

    E. "To me it means texture. This book has *pores* . . . . You'd find life under the glass, streaming past in infinite profusion."

    F. "We need not to be let alone. We need to be really bothered once in a while. How long is it since you were *really* bothered? About something important, about something real?"

    G. "A book is a loaded gun in the house next door . . . . Who knows who might be the target of the well-read man?"

    H. "The good writers touch life often. The mediocre ones run a quick hand over her. The bad ones rape her and leave her for the flies."

3. What is the main idea of the text below?

    "'Grandfather's been dead for all these years, but if you lifted my skull, by God, in the convolutions of my brain you'd find the big ridges of his thumbprint. He touched me. As I said earlier, he was a sculptor. 'I hate a Roman named Status Quo!' he said to me. 'Stuff your eyes with wonder,' he said 'live as if you'd drop dead in ten seconds. See the world. It's more fantastic than any dream made or paid for in factories.'"

    _____

    _____

4. Choose **two** supporting details from those below to support the main idea you identified in question 3.

    A. The parlor "families" can help the city people broaden their horizons.

    B. Nature holds wonders for personal growth and inspiration.

    C. Granger's grandfather believed each person should leave something significant behind when he or she died.

    D. Granger doesn't think Montag will understand what he is trying to say.

Comprehension Assessment (cont.)

5. Which statement best supports how Montag feels about Mildred?

   E. Montag doesn't want to live without Mildred.

   F. Montag thinks Mildred wants to make a better life for herself.

   G. Montag feels sorry for Mildred.

   H. Montag believes Mildred needs a life with her "family."

6. What is the meaning of the following text from *Dover Beach*?

   The Sea of Faith
   Ah, love, let us be true
   To one another! for the world, which seems
   To lie before us like a land of dreams,
   So various, so beautiful, so new,
   Hath really neither joy, nor love, nor light,
   Nor certitude, nor peace, nor help for pain;

   _____

   _____

7. Which statement best expresses a central theme of the book?

   A. People need the opportunity to fully explore their world and what it means to be human.

   B. To be an intellectual is the greatest achievement.

   C. It is ideal when the government is in control of its people.

   D. Avoiding controversial ideas and arguments can lead to a happier life.

8. What detail from the books provides the best evidence for your answer to number 7?

   E. "If you hide your ignorance, no one will hit you and you'll never learn."

   F. "The magic is only in what books say, how they stitched the patches of the universe together into one garment for us."

   G. "'Stuff your eyes with wonder,' he said, 'live as if you'd drop dead in ten seconds. See the world. It's more fantastic than any dream made or paid for in factories.'"

   H. "There must be something in books, things we can't imagine, to make a woman stay in a burning house; there must be something there. You don't stay for nothing."

Name _____

Date _____

Response to Literature: Alienation

Directions: The theme of alienation runs throughout *Fahrenheit 451*. The nation's people are alienated from books and ideas and nature. Montag and Mildred are alienated from one another. The learned, homeless men are alienated from their city. Discuss how Bradbury weaves this theme through the story. What concerns does he raise about the dystopian society he presents in the novel? What might Bradbury want us to notice in our current society? Explain your ideas with references to the text.

_____

_____

_____

_____

_____

_____

_____

_____

_____

_____

_____

_____

_____

_____

_____

Name _____

Date _____

Response to Literature Rubric

Directions: Use this rubric to evaluate student responses.

	Exceptional Writing	Quality Writing	Developing Writing
Focus and Organization	☐ States a clear opinion and elaborates well. Engages the reader from hook through the middle to the conclusion. Demonstrates clear understanding of the intended audience and purpose of the piece.	☐ Provides a clear and consistent opinion. Maintains a clear perspective and supports it through elaborating details. Makes the opinion clear in the opening hook and summarizes well in the conclusion.	☐ Provides an inconsistent point of view. Does not support the topic adequately or misses pertinent information. Provides lack of clarity in the beginning, middle, and conclusion.
Text Evidence	☐ Provides comprehensive and accurate support. Includes relevant and worthwhile text references.	☐ Provides limited support. Provides few supporting text references.	☐ Provides very limited support for the text. Provides no supporting text references.
Written Expression	☐ Uses descriptive and precise language with clarity and intention. Maintains a consistent voice and uses an appropriate tone that supports meaning. Uses multiple sentence types and transitions well between ideas.	☐ Uses a broad vocabulary. Maintains a consistent voice and supports a tone and feelings through language. Varies sentence length and word choices.	☐ Uses a limited and unvaried vocabulary. Provides an inconsistent or weak voice and tone. Provides little to no variation in sentence type and length.
Language Conventions	☐ Capitalizes, punctuates, and spells accurately. Demonstrates complete thoughts within sentences, with accurate subject-verb agreement. Uses paragraphs appropriately and with clear purpose.	☐ Capitalizes, punctuates, and spells accurately. Demonstrates complete thoughts within sentences and appropriate grammar. Paragraphs are properly divided and supported.	☐ Incorrectly capitalizes, punctuates, and spells. Uses fragmented or run-on sentences. Utilizes poor grammar overall. Paragraphs are poorly divided and developed.

The responses provided here are just examples of what students may answer. Many accurate responses are possible for the questions throughout this unit.

During-Reading Vocabulary Activity—Section 1: The First Half of Part One (page 16)

1. Clarisse is **earnest** because she is at once mysterious and observant. She is eager for conversation, social, and interested in people, ideas, and things.

2. The reader can't be sure why the Mechanical Hound flicks his **proboscis** and growls at Montag but should notice that Montag is suspicious that someone at the fire station has programmed the Hound to be sensitive to and aggressive toward Montag.

Close Reading the Literature—Section 1: The First Half of Part One (page 21)

1. Montag and Clarisse engage in personal conversation, asking each other thought-provoking questions and musing upon such topics as teen violence, school curriculum, having children, and what it means to be social.

2. The society holds that people are social if they play games and watch TV together and generally get along. By believing in all the same things and without examining differing perspectives on various issues, people will be happier.

3. Clarisse spends a lot of time with her family and by herself. She is interested in thinking and sharing about things she feels and observes in the world. Most teens in the story find entertainment through high-risk, sometimes violent, games and activities. They don't talk with one another.

4. Clarisse's uncle taught her about how people used to be. He says that kids didn't always kill each other and behave so recklessly. People used to be more responsible. Her uncle shares that art used to say something to people.

During-Reading Vocabulary Activity—Section 2: The Second Half of Part One (page 26)

1. Beatty explains to the **bewildered** Montag that the McClellans had long been on the watch list for antisocial behavior. They were considered problematic and possibly dangerous because they asked too many questions about why things are the way they are.

2. Architects stopped making front porches because such living space encouraged free time and conversation between people, something the government found to be **odious** and problematic for a happy society.

Close Reading the Literature—Section 2: The Second Half of Part One (page 31)

1. All but comic books and some magazines became illegal. Fireproof homes allowed a job change for firemen. Instead of putting out fires, they are charged with burning books. Beatty claims it was the people who called for this. People wanted to eliminate differing perspectives in order to be happier and live easier lives.

2. Mildred is visibly startled when she discovers the book. She asks about it aloud. Montag puts her off, and she leaves to turn on the parlor walls and her "family" in the other room.

3. According to Beatty, all people want to be happy and realize that the way to happiness is to level the playing field, making everyone the same. One way to do this is to remove all varying perspectives and controversial ideas.

4. The culture provides plenty of sporting events, games, and TV to keep people amused. The authorities burn up all unpleasant, disturbing things, including books and dead people. Most people seem content, except the outcasts like Clarisse, her uncle, and Montag.

Close Reading the Literature—Section 3: "The Sieve and the Sand" (page 41)

1. Faber admits to being a coward. He confesses that he never spoke up or issued a protest as book burning started.

2. According to Faber, to be happy, people need 1) books for their ideas, 2) time to wonder and consider ideas, and 3) the opportunity to act upon one's beliefs and desires.

3. People hate and fear books because they are confusing. So many perspectives are offered in different books that the range of ideas and philosophies overwhelms people, causing suffering and unhappiness.

4. In the flower metaphor, Faber is saying that we are trying to grow happiness out of the superficial. In order for real contentment in our humanity, we need substance, content that we can reckon with. People, like flowers, need nutritious soil in which to germinate sturdy stalks and blossoms.

During-Reading Vocabulary Activity—Section 4: The First Half of Part Three (page 46)

1. By hiding the book and calling the authorities, Montag is attempting to **rend** his relationship with the firemen, to sabotage the current paradigm, to shake things up, to challenge sensibilities, and to distract the police from his and Faber's escape.

2. The authorities strive to maintain ultimate power through the threat of death to criminals.

Close Reading the Literature—Section 4: The First Half of Part Three (page 51)

1. Mildred is frightened by Montag's recent attitude and behavior. She cannot understand him, has little relationship with him, and wants to save herself by leaving.

2. Beatty enumerates many beauties and fascinations with fire, including its purity and power, and as a natural element man wishes he invented. He asserts that fire is practical, cleansing, and mysterious. It destroys both responsibility and problems.

3. Bradbury uses dozens of striking similes and metaphors in this section, such as, "There was a crash like the falling parts of a dream fashioned out of warped glass, mirrors, and crystal prisms." This line suggests the shattering of disturbing human-made constructions.

4. Montag appears energized when he burns his house to the ground, seemingly intent on burning and demolishing all he has recently known. He exhibits a certain wild recklessness as he shoots the fire hose.

Close Reading the Literature—Section 5: The Second Half of Part Three (page 61)

1. Montag immerses himself in the river to escape from the Mechanical Hound, which is chasing him by scent, and to hide from the helicopters hunting for him. As he strips himself bare, there is also a suggestion that Montag is shedding his former shallow self, in preparation for taking on the challenge of ideas and a cultural revolution.

2. Montag feels comfort and peace in the river, a distinct shift from the violent razing of his home and his terrifying and death-defying flight from the city.

3. As he floats down the river taking in all the nature around him, Montag realizes that the sun and time do plenty of natural burning and that man needs to now preserve and archive what is worth saving. He sees that much is currently at stake and needs rescuing.

4. The smell of dry hay blowing reminds Montag of a farm he once visited. Remembering it, Montag is wishing for the opportunity to enjoy the comforts of nature and the human touch experienced through real, meaningful physical labor and care.

Comprehension Assessment (pages 67–69)

1. B. Books offer a range of ideas and perspectives, some conflicting.

2. G. "A book is a loaded gun in the house next door . . . . Who knows who might be the target of the well-read man?"

3. Make sure you have an impact on the world in which you live. On your path through life, be sure to change things and affect people.

4. B. Nature can hold wonders for personal growth and inspiration. C. Granger's grandfather believed each person should leave something significant behind when he or she died.

5. G. Montag feels sorry for Mildred.

6. Work together because the world out there is very tough for people alone.

7. A. People need the opportunity to fully explore their world and what it means to be human.

8. G. "'Stuff your eyes with wonder,' he said, 'live as if you'd drop dead in ten seconds. See the world. It's more fantastic than any dream made or paid for in factories.'"